War

Vancouver based writer and director, Dennis Foon is known both nationally and internationally for his contribution to innovative theatre for young people. In 1989 he received the International Arts for Young Audiences Award in recognition of his work. His many plays, which have been produced extensively throughout Canada and the world (translated into French, Danish, Hebrew, and Cantonese), include *The Short Tree and the Bird that Could Not Sing* (Chalmers Award), *Invisible Kids* (British Theatre Award), *New Canadian Kid*, *Mirror Game* (Blizzard), *Seesaw* (Blizzard), and *Skin* (Chalmers Award, Governor General's Finalist). Dennis was co-founder of Vancouver's Green Thumb Theatre where he was Artistic Director from 1975 to 1987. His screenplay, *Little Criminals*, is being produced by CBC-TV as a television feature film.

Other Blizzard plays by Dennis Foon
Seesaw
Mirror Game

WAR

by
Dennis Foon

Blizzard Publishing • Winnipeg

War first published 1995 by
Blizzard Publishing Inc.
73 Furby Street, Winnipeg, Canada R3C 2A2
© 1995 Dennis Foon

Photography © David Cooper
Cover art by Robert Pasternak.
Printed in Canada by Friesen Printers.

Published with the assistance of
the Canada Council and the Manitoba Arts Council.

Caution

Canadian Cataloguing in Publication Data

Foon, Dennis, 1951-

    War

    A play.
    ISBN 0-921368-53-4

I. Title.

PS8561.062W3 1995   C812'.54   C95-920113-0
PR9199.3.F66W3 1995

For E.

War was first produced by Green Thumb Theatre on school tour in British Columbia on October 3, 1994 with the following cast:

SHANE	Jacques Lalonde
TOMMY	Marcus Youssef
BRAD	Brock Johnson
ANDY	Camyar Chai

Directed by Guillermo Verdecchia
Choreographed by Barbara Bourget
Set and costumes by Kate King
Music by Alejandro Verdecchia
Stage managed by Michel Bisson

War was commissioned by Green Thumb Theatre, Patrick McDonald, Artistic Director; Peter Zednik, General Manager. It was workshopped with the assistance of Judith Mastai and the Vancouver Art Gallery. Many thanks to these organizations and the workshop participants (led by the uncompromising vision of Guillermo Verrdecchia) for their hard work and support.

I am particularly indebted to my dramaturge, Elizabeth Dancoes, for her insight and encouragement.

Playwright's Note

"Manhood training by its very nature creates the climate in which violence can flourish, and a society in which, despite its pious protestations, a level of violence is always tolerated, indeed expected. Boys will be boys."

—Rosalind Miles, *The Rites of Man*

I wrote *War* after going on the beat with the Vancouver Police, attending Youth & Violence conferences and seminars, speaking to social workers, youth workers, psychologists, teachers. I interviewed a hundred or so teens in public and alternate schools, group homes, drop-in centres, even two 15-year-olds who were handcuffed to chairs in the interrogation room—they'd just been arrested for beating another boy senseless.

Through those months, Rosalind Miles's words resonated. In fact, as Miles points out in her book, the expression "boys will be boys" is actually an imperative: boys must be boys.

The pressure to "be a man" is universal. Boys put it on boys, fathers put it on sons, men place it on men—repress feeling, be overly competitive, aggressive, invulnerable. This imperative was a common denominator linking all the males I interviewed. It skewered their ability to see themselves and the people (particularly women) around them clearly.

Bearing that in mind, I decided, for the first time, to write a play without female characters. In *War*, the women in the play are talked about and acted upon, but never seen. It's the not-seeing I was interested in exploring, the not-feeling.

Part of that disconnectedness is how we use language to reduce, disparage, and control others. That's also the reason I chose to invent a slang for the characters, to draw attention to the way we use words as weapons.

This provocative intention was quite effective, as the play was banned in one British Columbia school district on the basis of the volatility of its language. I was even asked to consider changing some of the words, which made this the first time I've experienced censorship of imaginary language. That particular incident did have a happy ending—the banning caused such a large outcry that the superintendent of those schools was forced to rescind the order.

A battle perhaps was won that day, but who wins the war is a question that each of us can only answer for ourselves.

Dennis Foon
1995

Preface

War is nothing but the continuation of
politics with the admixture of other means.
—Karl von Clausewitz

War is an ugly play. It is appalling, uncompromising, bleak. Unlike
so many plays for young audiences, *War* is not served up in a neat,
little, sugarcoated package with all conflicts resolved and a handy
moral thrown into the bargain. Foon takes his audience seriously;
therefore, *War* offers no easy comfort. There are no tidy solutions to
the problem of violence in our culture. Young people are aware of
this fact; they know all too well the complexity of the situation. To
pretend otherwise, and offer a tidy moral, a fable, would be a lie. It
would be irresponsible and *War*, in its bleakness, is a highly respon-
sible play. It is also, sadly, an accurate depiction of contemporary
social reality.

War does not pretend to be able to answer the problem of violence;
instead, it probes beneath the surface of the problem to reveal and
address some of its root causes. Foon's specific agenda here is an
examination of the construction of masculinity through violent behaviour and a disclosure of the disastrous consequences of that
praxis.

War presents us with four young persons, Tommy, Brad, Andy,
and Shane, all on the cusp of manhood, almost adults. Without excep-
tion, these man-boys live in a world where violence and violent
behaviour are expected and, what is more important, rewarded. Brad
and Andy have calculated the value of their aggression and their
futures look promising, at least from a material point of view. Brad
looks forward to "six figures" in his career as a professional hockey
player and Andy, modelling himself after Arnold Schwarzenegger,
Clint Eastwood, and Steven Seagal, hopes to earn not only millions of
dollars but also to "keep the power" by controlling the production of
his films.

The possibility that these two are deluded, or at least unrealistic, in their expectations does not matter. Both operate on the principle that "nothing in life is secure" and in order to survive, in daily and professional life, a man-boy must do "whatever it takes." In Brad's case, this credo means physically attacking other players ("Gouge your eyes ... smash nose into jelly") and tormenting his friend Tommy. Later, when he is demoted, precisely because of his aggressive behaviour (and his consequent lack of technical skill), his code of survival pushes him to commit arson: an act of revenge signalling a profound sexual disturbance. (Most pyromania is associated with sexual disorder.)

Shane, a former gang member, knows violence of all kinds can be lucrative. He is also familiar with the psychological rewards of violent behaviour. "It was like the sea parted when we walked in a room," he tells an entranced Andy. But Shane, unlike Andy, Tommy, and Brad, has seen the transitory nature of power built on aggression and dominance. He has witnessed his brother's death and his ignoble end, stuffed into a "drawer" and then a "box." Shane realizes, too late, that "the Hurt you put out stays alive ... and one day it finds you again."

Tommy's behaviour is not, it seems, motivated by pecuniary rewards. Instead, he seeks approval and power through violence. Beating up Andy, Tommy defends his tenuous status with Brad. Flying F-16's, Tommy hopes to achieve a kind of invincibility. "Nothing nothing touches you."

Where did these man-boys learn these hard lessons about life? They have built their survival codes out of scraps of information thrown to them along the way. Their attitudes seem to be imitations of behaviour condoned and glorified in the mass media, particularly television and film. These man-boys have no flesh-and-blood role models. The Coach and the Commander are distant figures who have arbitrary power over Tommy and Brad. According to Brad, it was the Coach who trained him "to smash and reap reward." It is this same coach who, inexplicably as far as Brad is concerned, demotes him and, the ultimate insult, replaces him with a young woman.

Parents barely figure in the play. Tommy never mentions a mother or a father. Brad makes only one reference to his father and that is a malicious joke. Sheila's parents are absent on the critical night of Tommy's attack. Shane never had a father, only a "Shank," who changed, it seems, on a monthly basis. It was one of these "Shanks" who initiated Shane and his brother into the world of violence at an early age. Of all the man-boys, Andy is the most verbose about his parents. But what does he say about them? His mother is "cracked for life" and his father is dead of "throat cancer that spread."

It is no coincidence that Andy's thoughts turn to his parents, his father in particular, moments before his showdown with Tommy and Brad. In such a moment of physical danger, a 17-year-old might well look for some instruction, some example of honourable comportment. But Andy's father is dead and Andy must guide himself with three mementos of his father: a note that reads "Be A Man" and two books: *The Joy of Sex* and *A Guide to Martial Arts.* Andy rightly senses that there is something of importance in these cryptic mementos but he cannot decipher the message they contain.

Foon is not bemoaning the absence of mothers and fathers in a mythopoetic "new-male" sense. These man-boys are literally lost in the world without anyone to assist them. They have inherited an absence, an emptiness. They have learned from an early age that survival, physical and emotional, depends on their capacity for not caring, not feeling. They are virtually incapable of showing affection or dealing with intimacy. Tommy claims he loved Sheila but Sheila insists he never called. Brad claims to be Tommy's pal but he consistently denigrates and humiliates him. Andy befriends Shane, yet, after Shane's death, renders the friendship in the terms of cost-benefit analysis: it was worth knowing him.

These man-boys are about to become men. Having nothing to rely on but the hollow postures they have acquired from popular culture, they will join the hundreds of thousands of hollow men in the world who lie, abuse, threaten, and kill.

***

In one of the most disturbing scenes of the play, Tommy describes, or narrates, his rape of his ex-girlfriend, Sheila. This particular scene is an excellent example of the potential contradiction that must be addressed if one is to represent violence without glorifying or revelling in it. (Many allegedly anti-violence films fall into this trap.) In Foon's play, Sheila is not present in the scene; there is no performer playing the role of Sheila. Instead, the audience is allowed into the hopelessly confused mind of the assailant while never forgetting the specific, horrible details of what is unfolding. We suffer for Sheila; we are horrified, revolted without the "spectacle" of rape. The playwright does not present us with an image of a powerless young woman subdued and brutalized by a man. (An image often repeated and exploited by commercial film and television for its emotional content.) In this way, Foon bypasses the entire problem of literally (or naturalistically) representing violence and allows us to come closer to the real problems of power and violence against women.

Those who object to this scene (and there have been objections) on the grounds that it offends moral sensibilities and shocks sensitive young minds, have not only their heads but their entire torsos buried in the sand. Eighty percent of all date rapes are perpetrated upon women; most of those women are between the ages of 13 and 24; eighty percent of those attacks occur in the victim's home; and, 67 % know their assailant.

***

If war is, as Clausewitz stated in his famous treatise on the subject, the continuation of politics by other means, what are the politics at the heart of this play? The politics that motivate the man-boys of *War* are the politics of power-over, the politics of domination. These are the same principles that spur the vicious corporate takeovers in the financial world. The very principles that inspire the war-makers of our world—the Reagans, Bushes and Thatchers. The same principles that drive the destruction of forests, lakes, and wildlife in the name of the free market and the pursuit of profit. It is precisely those politics that must be discontinued and unlearned if we are to survive collectively as human beings and not separately as winners and losers.

Foon has said that he wrote the play as a warning for his teenage daughter. Like all works of art, it transcends the immediate personal impulse that led to its creation and becomes a warning for all of us: mothers, fathers, children, adults, men, women. *War* warns us that continuing the politics of domination is literally a dead end. *War* warns us that we must look to ourselves to deal with the violence that surrounds and threatens to engulf us. *War* reminds us of the delicacy, the precariousness of our humanity (her name is Sheila) and it is that delicate, vulnerable humanity that we must nurture and fortify if we are to overcome the disaster we have made.

Guillermo Verdecchia
14 April, 1995
Vancouver

Characters

SHANE
TOMMY
BRAD
ANDY
They are all about 17-years-old.

The Set and Action

The play takes place in a variety of areas. It is not necessary to represent the locations naturalistically. The action of the play is meant to be continuous, without interuption for changes in setting.

Clockwise, left to right:
Andy (Camyar Chai); Shane (Jacques Lalonde);
Brad (Brock Johnson); Tommy (Marcus Youssef)
Photo by David Cooper

War

(The street. SHANE, dazed, blood on his t-shirt, enters.)

SHANE: *(To audience.)* I got in. Snuck in. I saw him. Saw what they were doing. Saw them finish. He's done up there now. They took him out. Put him somewhere else. Opened a drawer, put him in it. Tomorrow he goes out of the drawer. Into a box.

(Exercise room. BRAD pumps iron.)

TOMMY: Brad, man, she dumped me.

BRAD: You got dumped? By who?

TOMMY: Sheila. Who else.

BRAD: Sheila dumped you?

TOMMY: That's what I'm saying ... Why are you smiling?

BRAD: *(Smiling.)* I'm not smiling.

TOMMY: Yes you are, you're laughing, why are you laughing?

BRAD: 'Cause it's stupid.

TOMMY: Yeh, I know it's stupid. What's stupid?

BRAD: You hanging on to that skrunky piece till she gave you the heave.

TOMMY: She's no skrunk, I loved her man.

BRAD: I love 'em all, Tommy, but none of 'em, nobody, ever gives me the heave.

TOMMY: Well I've been heaved. Totally.

BRAD: Don't worry about it, Tom. Just don't let it happen again. I told you, always leave 'em begging for more. Then get on the next bus. Like I always say, Bud: pop 'em and chop 'em.

TOMMY: Yeh, right.

BRAD: Don't dog out on me, Tomster, it's bad sure, you got the chop. But at least you gave her the pop, right?

21

TOMMY: Yeh.

BRAD: You did pop the skrunk, didn't you?

TOMMY: ... Of course I did ... Like twenty times.

BRAD: Pretty good for one night.

TOMMY: Yeh, not bad.

BRAD: So what're you complainin' about?

TOMMY: I didn't just get chopped.

BRAD: More than chopped? What'd she do, man, B.F. you?

TOMMY: I've been B.F.'d major.

BRAD: Who'd she ditch you for?

TOMMY: You don't wanna know.

BRAD: I gotta know.

TOMMY: ... Andy.

BRAD: Andy? Big Andy the fullback? You're lucky she ran, man, that dude'd slice and dice you. What Big Andy wants, he takes and those of the living step aside.

TOMMY: It wasn't Big Andy.

BRAD: What other Andy is there?

TOMMY: The other Andy.

BRAD: ... The other Andy? She left you for the other Andy?

TOMMY: That's what I'm saying.

BRAD: You mean Andy the Scoob? He who acts in the school plays?

TOMMY: That's the perpetrator.

BRAD: That Andy doesn't even have pistons, Tom. He's not like onside, you know what I mean? Anyway, I thought that Andy was a tomato, you know, one of those.

TOMMY: So did I. Apparently Sheila's not in agreement.

BRAD: So what are you gonna do about it? What's gonna happen to Andy the Actor?

TOMMY: That's why I'm talking to you.

BRAD: What do you want me to do?

TOMMY: Help me out on this one, Brad.

BRAD: The guy's a feather man, just blow him over.

TOMMY: I'm not asking you to do anything, just back me up.

BRAD: Back up for what?

TOMMY: Just in case, you know, in case he has some.

BRAD: Tell me something, okay?

TOMMY: Sure, what?

BRAD: Would this make you feel better, you know, having a Bud there with you while you make the Scoob into turkey sausage?

TOMMY: It's nothing important, okay, I can go solo.

BRAD: I'll tell you what, you're my numero uno, right, Tommy?

TOMMY: That's right, and I'm with you too, Brad.

BRAD: So I'll be there. Not 'cause you need me or anything for this tomato squash thing, but for the company. I'll be like an observer, you know, all peace and love.

TOMMY: And if anything goes wrong?

BRAD: We bomb the shit out of them.

(They exit. A street near the school. SHANE enters.)

SHANE: *(To audience.)* There was this king. Everything he touched turned to gold. I used to love that story. Then I grew up. And everything I touched blew away.

(ANDY stands outside the school. SHANE observes, out of Andy's view.)

ANDY: *(Practicing.)*

Pretty princess primped and pricked the prone potatoes.

Prone potatoes pretty to primp she pricked and picked.

(To audience.)

My acting coach unloaded these diction exercises on me. Exercises your mouth. He says your head is one big resonator, like a stereo speaker. Use it! Use every square inch of your head! I thought he was demento till I found out he co-starred in two movies with Clint Eastwood. He's a close personal friend of Steven Spielberg. We even did screen tests that got sent down to him and critiqued. Spielberg, well, his executive assistant, said I had talent. My long-term plan is this: audition, audition, audition. Get on a TV show, like Johnny Depp did, do it for a few years, get the exposure, money in the bank, then into features. Co-star a lot, build up the rep, then start producing for myself. You produce it so you keep the profit. You keep the power. Schwarzenegger, Seagal, Costner, they control the product. Nobody pays them one million and walks away with a hundred and eighty. Eastwood takes half. Or more. Nothing in life is secure. But ninety million dollars would really help a lot, don't you think?

(TOMMY enters opposite SHANE and curiously watches ANDY from a distance as ANDY checks his text.)

ANDY: Whew, check the sibilant S: Sad Suzi Sanocane selling sautéed slivered cellophane.

(TOMMY approaches ANDY.)

TOMMY: Hey, very scary, Scoob.

ANDY: The name's Andy.

TOMMY: What's the rumble, Scoober?

ANDY: Diction exercises.

TOMMY: Diabolical.

ANDY: Right.

TOMMY: Don't jack me, bug head.

ANDY: Who's jacking?

TOMMY: You are. You're provoking my face.

ANDY: *(Getting ready to leave.)* I'll get out of it then, okay?

TOMMY: *(Giving ANDY a shove.)* Trespass.

ANDY: It was an error, I'm sorry.

TOMMY: *(Shoving him again.)* You're one big tactical error.

ANDY: Hey, get to the crux.

TOMMY: You. Nobody B.F.'s me.

ANDY: Sheila was no B.F. She said you two were kaput, you never call or see.

TOMMY: She was mine.

ANDY: We were just talk. She said you had no interest.

TOMMY: You want interest? Here.

(TOMMY hits ANDY in the stomach. ANDY goes down, winded. SHANE comes closer, watching.)

TOMMY: After school. In the cage.

(TOMMY exits. ANDY is still on the ground. Afraid of SHANE, he slowly rises as SHANE eyes him.)

ANDY: Do you want here? All yours. Just exiting.

(SHANE takes a step toward him.)

ANDY: Did I look at you? No offence intended.

(SHANE moves closer.)

ANDY: Truce, okay?

(Pause. SHANE takes a long look at ANDY.)

SHANE: Thought you were someone else.

ANDY: Who?

SHANE: Somebody.

ANDY: Anyone I know?

SHANE: ... No.

(SHANE exits. A locker room. BRAD puts on his hockey equipment. TOMMY helps.)

BRAD: *(To audience.)* I'm being scouted as we speak. For Junior A. I'll score the pros because whatever it takes, I do. Gouge your eyes, kick, spear, smash nose into jelly. That's the game. Get the advantage, get the big contract. I won't sign for less than six figures. Five years of pro, I'm set for life. 'Cause I know the secrets to success. Key: never apologize. Never a hint of weakness. You have to be totally sure about what you're doing. Listen to no one. Take no prisoners.

TOMMY: The Scoob is gumbo.

BRAD: Give it some color.

TOMMY: Absolutely check.

BRAD: Fracture his arm.

TOMMY: Done.

BRAD: Leg?

TOMMY: Crutches.

BRAD: How you gonna do this deed?

TOMMY: I'm combat trained.

BRAD: Exam. Show me how you bust an arm.

TOMMY: Now?

BRAD: *(Holding out his arm.)* Yeah, here. Break it.

TOMMY: I'm not gonna bust your arm.

BRAD: Are you snubbing a formal invite?

TOMMY: You gotta do practice.

BRAD: Test your weapons. Take the arm.

TOMMY: *(Taking it.)* I took it.

BRAD: Very good. Step Two.

TOMMY: Twist it?

BRAD: Be my guest.

> *(TOMMY starts to twist BRAD's arm.)*

BRAD: Tommy, a bone is like a stick. Yay thick. How do you crack a stick?

TOMMY: Put it on a rock and jump on it.

> *(He places his arm on the bench.)*

BRAD: Rock. Go.

TOMMY: But this is your arm, not the Scoober's.

BRAD: Pretend.

TOMMY: I'll hurt you.

BRAD: Pain's a state of mind. Haven't you learned that yet in the cadets, Corporal?

TOMMY: *(Hotly.)* You want me to jump? I'm jumping.

> *(TOMMY gets into position.)*

BRAD: Bombs away.

> *(TOMMY jumps. BRAD pulls his arm away at the last second. TOMMY falls into a heap.)*

TOMMY: Why'd you move it?

BRAD: Lesson One: Always stay alert, soldier. *(Picking up his stick.)* See you in the cage.

> *(They exit. The cage. ANDY, with headphones on and a book opened nearby, follows the instructions he hears.)*

MASTER LIANG: *(Voice over.)* From open palm, fold fingers. Place thumb on top of index and middle fingers. See illustration 5B.

> *(ANDY refers to the book.)*

ANDY: Sad fact: I have to read a book to learn how to make a fist.

MASTER LIANG: *(Voice over.)* Keep wrist even with forearm ... Weight on right foot, lunge forward and punch. Punch.

> *(ANDY does, awkwardly. He takes off the headphones.)*

ANDY: *(To audience.)* This is the cage. Just a fence really. In about half an hour everybody will pour out of class to see the bloodbath. My blood bath. A hundred kids'll be hanging off the chainlink. Very old Rome, our version of the colosseum and gladiators. In this case I'm the bait they're throwing to the lions. I'm not completely unprepared, though. See? *(He picks up the book.)* Master *Liang's Guide to Martial Arts* with Master Liang's actual voice on cassette. A present from my dad before he died. This and *The Joy of Sex.* We never discussed either subject when I was growing up. Then about two years ago, he got throat cancer that spread and had about a month to live.

Everybody was a big mess about it, my mom still is, all she does is cry and pray all day, she's definitely cracked for life. Anyway, for me the whole thing was a dream. Didn't feel a thing, kinda like being stoned, floating in a daze. I just zombied through it all, like my eyes were crossed or something.

Then one day I do the hospital for a visit and he hands me this book with cassette. And *The Joy of Sex.* Like it was a little late, you know what I mean? Most guys learn these things from an early age. But not me. My dad was never around. Always on the road. Or reading newspapers. I saw more of him that last month in the hospital than I did my whole life. And even then it wasn't like we had long conversations. After all, he didn't have a throat. But he'd write me profound little notes.

This is my favorite one. Took him about ten minutes to write it 'cause he was so wiped from the morphine. Says "Be a Man." That's the whole thing. Be a Man. I forgot to ask him how you do that. But even if I did ask, he wasn't talking. I guess he figured everything you need to know on the subject is summed up in these two books. Anyhow he died a day after writing this note. So I guess he thought it was pretty important.

(ANDY puts down the book and practices his punches. TOMMY and BRAD appear.)

BRAD: Hey, it's Mr. Kung Fu.

ANDY: You're early.

TOMMY: No, you are. Is this a jack? An ambush? You got a black belt or something?

ANDY: Fourth Degree.

TOMMY: He says he's diploma'd in black belt.

BRAD: So do I, Tommy. Here, take my diploma.

(BRAD takes off his studded leather belt and gives it to TOMMY.)

BRAD: You know, Tommygun, I think this cantaloupe lacks back up.

ANDY: They're coming.

BRAD: This pumpkin is one big lack.

(TOMMY stalks around ANDY, who backs away.)

TOMMY: Come on, explicate a black belt to me.

ANDY: Fair means we wait.

TOMMY: Maybe I'll show you.

(TOMMY flicks the belt at him a few times. He connects. He flicks it again. ANDY reaches out and grabs it away.)

TOMMY: Hey, give it.

ANDY: Nay.

BRAD: That's my personal wardrobe, Scoober.

TOMMY: Return the item.

ANDY: For a truce.

BRAD: My belt for your life?

ANDY: Correct.

BRAD: Scooby Doober drives hard bargain, Tom.

TOMMY: All you do is get in my face.

BRAD: He imagines his life has more value than my belt.

TOMMY: He imagines he's God.

BRAD: I paid sixty bucks for this belt. And he wants even trade. Oh, I hate being jacked.

(BRAD's arm jets out. He grabs ANDY by the back of the neck. ANDY winces with pain.)

Give me what's mine.

(ANDY hands over the belt.)

BRAD: Continue. Interest. You owe me.

ANDY: Take what you want.

BRAD: I want everything.

(TOMMY strips Andy's jacket off him. Hands it to BRAD.)

Persevere.

On the left: Andy (Camyar Chai); on the right: Tommy (Marcus Youssef)
Photo by David Cooper

ANDY: I just got these.

(TOMMY slaps him. ANDY takes off his shoes.)

BRAD: Additional.

(TOMMY slaps him again. ANDY takes off his pants. He's down to his underwear.)

BRAD: Gee, I'm starting to feel shopped out. What time is it, Scoob?

(ANDY looks at his watch, then gets the message.)

ANDY: My dad gave this to me.

BRAD: He has wonderful taste.

TOMMY: Give it.

ANDY: No.

TOMMY: You deaf or what?

ANDY: You can't have.

(TOMMY tries to grab it. ANDY won't let it go. TOMMY puts him in a neck squeeze. ANDY, suffocating, lets TOMMY take the watch.TOMMY hands it to BRAD.)

BRAD: A work of art.

(He drops the watch and crushes it under his foot.)

ANDY: No!

(He charges at BRAD, who slugs him.)

BRAD: All yours, Tombo.

TOMMY: Thanks.

(TOMMY starts to pummel ANDY, who falls to the ground.)

BRAD: We shop, he drops.

(BRAD looks up and is startled to see SHANE is standing there.)

BRAD: *(Nervously.)* Greetings, Shane. Here for the show?

SHANE: ... I'm his back up.

BRAD: ... Welcome. Gotta go.

(BRAD drops Andy's jacket and takes off.)

TOMMY: Hey Brad—

(He watches BRAD exiting, and looks at SHANE, then nervously runs off. ANDY, trembling, humiliated, puts his jeans back on.)

SHANE: You okay?

ANDY: I'd like to 86 that guy.

SHANE: No you wouldn't.

ANDY: He was messing me for a girl I'm just friends with.

SHANE: Ain't it the way. *(Picks up the crushed watch and hands it to ANDY.)* Pretty wasted.

ANDY: No matter. Just sentimental value.

SHANE: That's worth something.

ANDY: Not really.

SHANE: More than you think.

ANDY: ... Didn't expect somebody like you by the cage.

SHANE: I'm out of it.

ANDY: You quit your gang? The TMR?

SHANE: No one ever quits.

ANDY: Shane ... Thanks for the back up.

(ANDY, finished dressing, runs off.)

SHANE: *(To audience.)* I had good back up once. Best in the world. He'd take it for me, or me for him, whatever kept us alive. Since we were three, four, five. The Shank'd come home tanked, bust us up. Once, I was twelve, Shank was slamming my face in the wall, painting the plaster red. My back up pressed his butt with my mom's hot iron. It worked. He let go. No matter who the Shank was that month we'd stand up together. Pay the price together. Be the eyes in back each others' head. We had to. We were brothers.

(SHANE exits. Tommy's room. TOMMY is putting on his uniform. BRAD watches.)

BRAD: Your juicer the Scoob has quality back up.

TOMMY: The guy's a tomato, where'd he score the army? Wasn't that Shane playing in the big murder thing that happened?

BRAD: That's the man.

TOMMY: He's lethal. What was he doing with Scoob?

BRAD: Evidently they're friends.

TOMMY: Did you see how he eyed me. Cold like a butcher ready to cut.

BRAD: You're some slab of beef.

TOMMY: I hate being scanned like that.

On the left, sitting: Shane (Jacques Lalonde); on the right, sitting: Brad (Brock Johnson); standing on the chairs; Tommy (Marcus Youssef); standing to the right: Andy (Camyar Chai)
Photo by David Cooper

BRAD: Bangers at Shane's level do whatever they want. Their life is in balance.

TOMMY: Eyeballs popping to strangle me is no balance.

BRAD: He's scoping the size of your major veins and arteries. Sussing the best place to slice.

TOMMY: I could take him down.

BRAD: You're a very twisted guy. It's an attractive quality.

TOMMY: Thank you.

BRAD: You're welcome.

(BRAD exits.)

TOMMY: *(To audience.)* Art of survival. That's what the military's all about. Dodging shells. Weapons handling. Search and rescue. Freeing hostages with gunships. Next year I move to the Island to train as a fighter pilot. I'll be flying F-16s. See the world. At twice the speed of sound. Once you're strapped in, you're the jet, the jet's you. Not virtual reality. Reality reality. It's you. You plug into it. Become One. The oxygen, the communications. Computer at your fingertips. Only now, you're not this. This weakness. This nothing. Now your skin is Titanium. Your ears are enhanced radar. Your eyes are infra-red thermal sights. You move stratospheric. You have smart bombs, glide bombs, Maverick missile-seeker heads. Boom. You hit the speed of sound once. Boom. You hit it twice. And you keep going. You're passing one thousand two hundred miles an hour, one thousand three hundred, four hundred, five hundred. And nothing nothing touches you.

(TOMMY, in uniform, exits. The street. BRAD approaches ANDY.)

BRAD: Andy.

ANDY: Andy?

BRAD: I was speaking your name. I just wanted to say sorry for all that.

ANDY: You're sorry.

BRAD: These things happen, you know. Unfortunate. Still harbour the watch?

ANDY: What about it?

BRAD: The repair is mine.

ANDY: Pass.

BRAD: I got a trifle worked up. Ditto to the rink. A puck or a stick in your face, click. You smash a jaw, you break a watch, nez pa?

ANDY: Slightly.

BRAD: Let me examine. Please.

(ANDY takes the watch out of his pocket and reluctantly hands it to BRAD)

BRAD: It's beautiful. It's old. Is it rare?

ANDY: It meant something to me.

BRAD: From dead Dad, no?

ANDY: Correct.

BRAD: My dad? Not dead. Yet. Let me get this fixed.

ANDY: No.

BRAD: It was collateral damage. I'll fix it. War reparations.

ANDY: I don't think so.

BRAD: *(Pocketing the watch.)* I'm doing this for you. Breaking gifts from dead fathers is shameful. I'm ashamed. You see, I want friendship.

ANDY: I don't think so.

BRAD: I understand your hesitation. We can take it slow. No rushing in. Gradually you'll see me as a person. Give me a chance. Okay?

ANDY: *(After a pause.)* Okay.

BRAD: So how many moons you been souling with Shane?

ANDY: Is that what this is about?

BRAD: No, it's just chitty chat. Breaking the ice. How long?

ANDY: … Long enough.

BRAD: Have you done battle with him before?

ANDY: *(Lying.)* Whenever necessary.

BRAD: Tell me, is he vengeful?

ANDY: As in, is he going to cut the bones out of your hands?

BRAD: For example.

ANDY: You'll have to ask him. Then again, you could just cut your hands off and save him the trouble.

BRAD: Humour. Anytime you need back up, Andy, let me know. I'm right behind you. I mean that.

ANDY: Thanks.

BRAD: I'll have your Dad's watch for you A.M.

   (BRAD exits. SHANE enters. ANDY runs up to him.)

ANDY: This was premium suckholing. High octane grovelling. He fears you deeply.

SHANE: No reason to.

ANDY: You have a terrifying reputation, you know. People think you're a killer.

SHANE: Oh yeah?

ANDY: Are you? *(Quickly backing off.)* My agent phoned.

SHANE: Agent?

ANDY: For TV, movies. I'm up for a part.

SHANE: Gro.

ANDY: I play a gangbanger.

SHANE: You?

ANDY: Real. He said I look like one.

SHANE: No you don't.

ANDY: Don't spill to the producers. If I score, it's 500 a day. Minimum.

SHANE: Who do you have to waste?

ANDY: Nobody. I act.

SHANE: That's check.

ANDY: But first I have to score the part. Will you help?

SHANE: I can't act.

ANDY: Coach me. Make me real.

SHANE: Not possible.

ANDY: *(Imitating him.)* Not possible.

SHANE: Gimp.

ANDY: That's why you gotta teach me.

SHANE: Teach what?

ANDY: The works. What you do.

SHANE: Are you a rat?

ANDY: No, I swear it. Research.

SHANE: I told you, I'm not doing crime.

ANDY: Then just teach me The Thing.

SHANE: What is The Thing?

ANDY: The no fear. The death eyes. The you-never-get-messed-with.

SHANE: You think I have this?

ANDY: That's what you are. Totally. Either you were born that way or you learned it.

SHANE: Learned what?

ANDY: Everything. Standing up for yourself.

SHANE: You just do it.

ANDY: That's it. That's what I can't do. It. Can't Just Do It.

SHANE: I saw you act. You can do anything.

ANDY: Sure, on the stage. But it's fake, not real life. They all know it and waste me. I want them to look at me like they look at you.

SHANE: No you don't.

ANDY: Yes I do.

> *(SHANE shakes his head. They both exit. Outside schoolyard. BRAD and TOMMY enter.)*

BRAD: *(To audience.)* So I head to practice. Coach says com'ere talk. Has that look on his face. I'm thinking: who died? Turns out: me. Demoted. Fourth Line. Why? I'm a walking penalty. With me, game can't flow. New blood required. Fresh improved model. Charlie Norris. Skates like Gretsky. Stickhandles like Howe. Major asset. Makes it flow. Who is this Charlie Norris I ask, filled with curiosity. You know her, he says. Charlene. And then I know. I'm replaced by a she. A skrunk. I'm bumped for a skrunk. This is a joke, right? You're skrunking me, he who pours blood for the team. She can't check. She can't spear. She can't gouge. But no, says he, we don't want that anymore. We require finesse. Since I'm seven-years-old he and his buds train me to smash and reap reward. For ten years I'm their sluggo man. And today I'm slagged. For a skrunk. Is this justice?

TOMMY: *(TOMMY goes to BRAD.)* The commander weirded out on me.

BRAD: The psycho soldier.

Brad (Brock Johnson)
Photo by David Cooper

TOMMY: He says our troops go with the UN. We don't make war, we make peace. I'd only get to fly an F-16 for surveillance.

BRAD: The UN torched Iraq.

TOMMY: That woulda been premium, dropping twenty-five hundred pound Glide Bombs. Boom, boom, boom: three square blocks. But most days it's different. Like we're keeping the peace some place in Europe or Africa, you know, some country, our soldiers smacked in a civil war.

BRAD: No shooting?

TOMMY: Yeah, there's shooting all over the place.

BRAD: Elegant.

TOMMY: But not us, we don't get to. On one side, they're called the Wandis or Snergs or something, they don't want our soldiers delivering food to the other side. So they take pot shots at our guys. They know we can't return fire.

One time a bunch of Snergs surround a dozen of our troops. Our guys don't fight back, just plop down their weapons. The Snergs are laughing and everything, right? Say they're gonna execute them. So our boys are lined up against the wall, shaking and praying. The Snergs aim their rifles. Bang! But nobody drops. The bullets smack into the wall above their heads. Our guys are stunned, like what happened? And there are the Snergs, rolling on the ground, laughing their brains out.

BRAD: Did our boys come back in tanks and nuke the clowns?

TOMMY: That's what I thought, right? Like we got Colt 16A2's, we got Barrett 50 Caliber Armour Piercers, let's smoke the smeggers.

BRAD: Skrunk those Snergs.

TOMMY: So guess what? We can't.

BRAD: What're you talking about?

TOMMY: The commander said our orders are peace. No matter how primo the provoking, no firing back. He said those soldiers were right surrendering their weaponry and letting the Snergs wank away. If we shoot back, we join the problem. All violence does is make more violence, he states.

BRAD: For this you gave up half your life?

TOMMY: I been in cadets forever.

BRAD: They lie. All of them lie. You walking?

TOMMY: I wanna fly an F-16.

BRAD: You'll never fly it. You'll never be it.

TOMMY: I could. Maybe.

BRAD: You been skrunked.

TOMMY: The commander says they're heroes.

BRAD: For letting those Croaks wilt their wieners?

TOMMY: For being unprovoked.

BRAD: If you think that's match, you swallow.

TOMMY: F-16.

BRAD: Flying gunless bombless gutless.

TOMMY: Still got speed.

BRAD: You got nothing. They took it all!

> *(BRAD turns away from TOMMY.)*

BRAD: *(To audience.)* Terrible thing happened at the rink. Everybody skating like angels, sweating buckets to gain finesse, stickhandling like Swedes, gliding between each other with dainty little air pockets between us. Coach all Gandhi smiles 'cause it's flowing, its flow flow flow. But then a little scent. A smell. Could this be smoke? Alarm! Panic. Evacuation! Everybody's outside, shaking in skates, watching firefighters hose down the locker room. This is bad, this could do the season. This could place the coach on waivers. Sadly, his new star seems to play with matches. Her locker filled with inflammables ignited torching the contents. All is charred and cindered. Nothing is left. Hockey is dead.

> *(He lights a match. ANDY and SHANE rush on, playing at kickboxing.)*

SHANE: Lift that leg, higher!

ANDY: I'm permanently damaged.

SHANE: Block!

> *(SHANE expertly kicks at ANDY's face. He blocks it.)*

ANDY: Hah!

SHANE: Again!

ANDY: No more.

> *(The kick comes. ANDY blocks again.)*

SHANE: Don't quit!

Slumped over, left to right: Shane (Jacques Lalonde) and Andy (Camyar
Chai); foreground, sitting: Brad (Brock Johnson)
Photo by David Cooper

(Another kick. ANDY blocks it and then collapses, laughing.)

SHANE: Good reflexes.

ANDY: I'm sausage meat. You could coach you know, you're great at this.

SHANE: Uh huh.

ANDY: Seriously, my agent could gig you. We could do shoots together.

SHANE: Shoots?

ANDY: Extras on movie sets. You'd trip it.

SHANE: Possible prime.

ANDY: Definite prime. Will you do it?

SHANE: *(After a pause.)* Why not?

ANDY: Alright!

(They slap hands.)

ANDY: *(To audience.)* I got an authentic banger on side! An actual maim, pillage and destroyer! He's a true psycho man. He knows the land. That's what the shows want. Real. And real means the edge. I got real. I score!

(TOMMY and BRAD continue talking.)

TOMMY: F-16.

BRAD: You couldn't take down a tomato. How're you gonna take up a fighter?

TOMMY: F-16's are computer. You use keyboard.

BRAD: And catheter.

TOMMY: What?

BRAD: I read. No toilets in those things. You leak into a tube, goes in plastic bag. One pilot, 20,000 feet up, tries changing bag. It slips. Piss spills all over the computer. It sparks, short circuits. The plane goes into spin. He ejects. Coming down the pee bag freezes, bangs him in face, out cold, hits the ground, breaks his neck. Killed by his own piss.

TOMMY: B.S.

BRAD: True story. Just like you. Mr. Premature Ejection.

TOMMY: One laser guided rocket could take out this whole school.

One round from the machine gun'd 86 every teacher. One smart
bomb'd vaporize the works.

BRAD: You're provoked.

TOMMY: No. Not.

BRAD: No control.

TOMMY: I do. I have. Commander gave us exercises. Practice.

BRAD: You mean, breathing and talking to yourself?

TOMMY: Self talk. Guided breath.

BRAD: Oh, science. I'll practice you.

TOMMY: You really want to?

BRAD: Sure. I tell you stuff. You be a good UN soldier.
You're the one who wants to fly.

TOMMY: Alright.

BRAD: Guess my agenda last night.

TOMMY: Went out?

BRAD: Saw a friend. Of yours.

TOMMY: Who?

BRAD: Beautiful Sheila.

TOMMY: What?

BRAD: Are you breathing?

TOMMY: Yeah.

BRAD: I parachuted into her place. Her parents were absent.

TOMMY: You're making this up.

BRAD: You decide, soldier. She invited me. She wearing robe at
the door.

TOMMY: She closes people out if nobody's home.

BRAD: First time she said. Self talk, Toto.

TOMMY: First what?

BRAD: First everything. First tour of the solar system. Mars, Mer-
cury, and Venus. Touched every planet.

TOMMY: I doubt you.

BRAD: Are you breathing?

TOMMY: Yes I'm breathing.

BRAD: She said you never performed any of that stuff with her. Said you tried once but failed.

TOMMY: She never said that.

BRAD: She's a biter, man, she screams.

TOMMY: You're lying.

BRAD: Right on her parents' bed. Hey, note the hickey.

TOMMY: No way!

(TOMMY rushes at BRAD, who pins him.)

BRAD: Tommy, breathe. Be a hero. Don't let yourself be provoked.

TOMMY: If you touched her ...

BRAD: Think F-16. Think flying high over clouds, bursting speed of sound, criss-crossing the globe.

TOMMY: How could you?

BRAD: Curiosity. Could I maintain over an hour? Yes.

TOMMY: You touched her.

BRAD: I'm not rude. I accept invitations.

TOMMY: I'll kill you!

BRAD: Sorry, Bud, you just crashed the test. Better luck next year, Corporal.

TOMMY: ... I thought you were my Bud.

BRAD: I am.

(TOMMY storms off. ANDY does another kick for SHANE.)

ANDY: Where'd you catch this, anyway?

SHANE: Along the trail.

ANDY: Your whole life?

SHANE: Sure.

ANDY: First fight.

SHANE: Don't remember.

ANDY: Biggest fight.

SHANE: All big.

ANDY: Most important.

SHANE: Grade seven. Robert Flowers.

ANDY: Get out.

SHANE: A giant. He challenges. I win. Then all the big ones challenge. I beat them all. Or my brother does. Then we get offers.

ANDY: To beat people up?

SHANE: Like a big cousin coming for revenge. We'd take him for fifteen bucks. Or hired to dive a playground and smash somebody.

ANDY: Like bam in the face?

SHANE: Like bambambambam. For ten, twenty bucks, whatever they had.

ANDY: What did they do?

SHANE: I don't know, we just beat them up.

ANDY: Is this with TMR?

SHANE: *(Chilled.)* Never. I'm talking pre-TMR. This is way before that. This is nothing with TMR. Zero.

ANDY: Okay. We never talked TMR. Ever. Hey!

> *(Trying to lighten the mood, ANDY does some kicks. SHANE ignores him.)*

SHANE: I'm gone.

ANDY: Shane ... what's the static? Where are you?

SHANE: *(Pause. Eyes ANDY.)* You know what a shadow is?

ANDY: As in where the sun's blocked, the light can't get through?

SHANE: ... Yeah, no light.

ANDY: I don't get it, Shane. Shane?

> *(SHANE exits. TOMMY sits on a chair.)*

TOMMY: I walked. Couldn't stop thinking it. Since High School, Brad's been my number one. B.F. me? No. A Scoob'd do that. An anybody. Not Brad. Not unless she gave the open highway. If she really opened that door. He couldn't say no if the table was set. Rain started. Couldn't feel it. Kept walking. The sun dies, darkness begins.

I come to this street. Familiar. Focus my eyes. I see it. Her house. I robot to the door. Stare at it. How long? Forever. Then I reach. Watch my finger touch the bell. Ring. Nothing. Ring. Hear footsteps. Behind the curtain I'm looked at by a shadow. It's her. I say, hi, Sheila, here I am. She pauses. Tommy? Yeah. I missed you. It's late, the shadow says, nobody's home. That's okay, the robot says back. I just. Wanna talk.

Tommy (Marcus Youssef)
Photo by David Cooper

Click. Door opens. Sheila. Standing there. In a robe. I go to kiss
her. She stops me. You said you just wanted to talk. Chit-chat,
okay? So we chitty-chat for twenty-five thousand hours. Then it
pukes out of me like a stone: Did you and Brad? She turns red.
You never call or see. Then you come. And ask that? Yes, I say.
Did you do Brad? Now she's even redder. Angry. None of your
business.

Business. None of mine. I feel my insides turning steam. Turning
burning. None of my business. What did you do to him? Nothing.
How did he touch you? He didn't. How did you touch him? Get
out, she says. I take her hand. She pulls away. But I don't let go.
She let him in like she never let me, loved him like me never. She
was gonna love me now. But she's no. Not me. Not good enough
me. But me knows you. Me knows you everything. What you did.
What you did. What you did. What you did!

Then it was over. She's crying. Softly. I ask if I was as good. No
answer. Try to kiss her goodbye but she turns her head. So I left.

I guess she phoned on me. That's how I'm here. Do I get to make
a phone call?

*(He tries to stand. One of his wrists is handcuffed to the chair.
Near the cage. BRAD approaches ANDY.)*

BRAD: Dad's watch, Andy. Healed.

(ANDY takes it. Listens.)

ANDY: Ticks.

BRAD: Reborn. So what's the traffic you and Shane?

ANDY: Usual. Tommy?

BRAD: Don't know what got into the boy, messing up Sheila
like that.

ANDY: She's out of hospital.

BRAD: She'll live. Tombo's released today too.

ANDY: Till the trial.

BRAD: Where's Shane?

ANDY: Out picking flowers.

BRAD: I don't get him. Had it all and walked from it.

ANDY: How do you mean?

BRAD: The cars, the clothes. He was moving. Him and his brother had wings.

ANDY: You know his brother?

BRAD: Gunned down in some premium firefight.

ANDY: What's the interest, Brad?

BRAD: I wouldn't mind being cut in.

ANDY: Into what?

BRAD: Into whatever you guys got going.

ANDY: We got nothing going.

BRAD: That's my point. This guy carries major rank and walks TMR. He must have a side effect. And you're in on it. What did you find him?

ANDY: You're asking nice?

BRAD: I'm pleading.

ANDY: I found him somebody.

BRAD: What?

ANDY: An agent.

BRAD: An arranger? A halfwayer?

ANDY: Affirmed. The agent's gonna get us some shoots.

BRAD: I could like that. Let me in.

ANDY: Why digress from hockey.

BRAD: Screw hockey. Hockey's smeg.

ANDY: But you're the guy.

BRAD: Hockey's scabbed. It's pus. I want with you.

ANDY: Problem: trust.

BRAD: Test.

ANDY: Now?

BRAD: Now.

(ANDY gives this some thought.)

ANDY: The belt.

BRAD: This belt?

ANDY: The black belt.

(BRAD takes it off. ANDY snaps it, testing it.)

BRAD: Where?

ANDY: Make some space.

(BRAD takes off his jacket.)

ANDY: Continue.

BRAD: Right here?

ANDY: Affirmed.

(BRAD takes off his shirt.)

ANDY: Persevere.

(BRAD points to his shoes. ANDY nods.)

ANDY: Additional.

BRAD: Are you maxing me?

ANDY: So it appears.

(BRAD strips down to his underwear.)

BRAD: And more?

ANDY: Nay. At ease.

BRAD: What's the plan?

(ANDY flicks the belt in the air. BRAD winces.)

ANDY: We'll be in touch.

(ANDY tosses the belt to BRAD and exits, smiling. BRAD, covering himself up, exits too. Late at night. SHANE slowly crosses the stage and taps on Andy's bedroom window. He enters the room; ANDY is asleep.)

SHANE: *(Shaking him.)* Andy ... Andy.

ANDY: What time is it?

SHANE: Late.

ANDY: You look like crap. What happened?

SHANE: It's coming back around.

ANDY: What is?

SHANE: Here today, gone tomorrow.

ANDY: You're cold. Here's a blanket.

SHANE: You tucking me in?

(ANDY laughs.)

ANDY: Nay.

SHANE: You laugh like him.

ANDY: Your brother?

SHANE: Same. And eyes. He once told me the clock was ticking. That the Hurt we put out would come back on us. Like Karma.

ANDY: What did he mean?

SHANE: He was stoned, reading it in a comic book. I was ripped, couldn't stop giggling when he said it. Nothing was gonna catch up with us. We were so high no one could take us down. Sometimes we made six hundred bucks a day. Once we scored a thousand. We didn't ask questions. If they said torch this building or trash this car or kick this guy's head in, we did it. Better than anybody. We were mutants, man. We had the power to smash, blast and explode. It was like the sea parted when we walked in a room. If we wanted something, we just took it. You know what that feels like? To be all-powerful?

Then it happened. Don't know how. Some guy, a wannabe. What'd he want? I wannabe you. I wannabe in. I get in if I get you out. Something like that. It was a dance, a bunch of us hanging out front, smoking, snorting whatever. Feeling great. We were joking about smashing the Shank's teeth out, then giving him the money for the dentist. The wannabe comes up to us, grinning. Pulls out this long bread knife, one of those flimsy things from a dollar store with a plastic handle. Like ooo we're scared man, we were cracking up. The kid was laughing too, nervous like ... And then he slides it into my brother's gut.

My brother hardly felt it. Like a sting. Pulls it out and starts chasing the little punk with it. Never saw him run so fast, he was pissed, who was this bug anyway? Finally he corners the kid. Grabs his ear. Nice earring he says. And cuts it off. The kid screams, didn't know how lucky he was. Then my brother falls, passes right out.

I went in the ambulance with him. He wasn't talking. Just staring out in space. Don't know if he could hear me. The doctors kept me downstairs at the hospital. Wouldn't let me know what was going on. Till finally I just said screw this and snuck into a closet, put on an orderly's gown. Took the elevator up to the operating room. I wanted to know what was happening, but it couldn't be bad. It was

Shane (Jacques Lalonde)
Photo by David Cooper

a puny bread knife, sticker still on it, a buck and a half at the store. My brother hardly felt it, what could it do?

I came out the elevator into a hallway. Through the glass I could see all the nurses and doctors huddled around this guy on the operating table. He was cut open from his neck to his crotch. The skin and ribs spread right apart. You could see all his insides. Heart, lungs, intestines. All of it.

And them with the tubes and sponges and needles, trying to stitch up wherever that knife had sliced. He looked something like my brother but it wasn't him. It was this guy with grey skin. Grey like a raining sky. Only it wasn't raining water. The floor was covered in red. All their feet turned red from walking in it. Like a dam burst in that room, a flood, filling up with my brother's blood.

At the funeral, he looked really nice. Sewed him all together, put him in a suit, lots of makeup. Hair combed nice. This lady came up to me, said he looked serene. He did look kinda peaceful. But all I could see was that grey face staring, chest split open, and that ocean of red that came out of him for a buck forty-nine.

ANDY: I'm sorry.

SHANE: Nothing to do with you. He took it. Now it's my turn.

ANDY: You worry too much.

SHANE: The Hurt you put out stays alive. Floats in the air, drifting around for weeks, months, years. And one day, any day, finds you again. Doesn't care if you're bad or good now. Just smells you and splatters your life away. That's how it works.

ANDY: You're shivering. The blanket.

(ANDY adjusts it. He sees something.)

ANDY: Shane, what is this?

SHANE: The Hurt found me.

ANDY: This looks bad.

SHANE: Not so.

ANDY: Don't move. I'm gonna get you help. Hang on, Shane.

SHANE: You worry too much.

(At the cemetary. TOMMY and BRAD enter in funeral clothes.)

TOMMY: Lawyer says two years YDC. And two probation.

BRAD: How'd the commander read?

TOMMY: Won't recommend me to fly. No F-16.

BRAD: Ouch. What now?

TOMMY: I can enlist on release. But infantry.

BRAD: There's still the premium weaponry.

TOMMY: I have to stay on the ground.

BRAD: Cannons, tanks, grenade launchers.

TOMMY: I just wanted to fly.

BRAD: Check. *(Pause.)* ... You know I never touched her.

TOMMY: Yes you did.

BRAD: You're crazy.

TOMMY: You put skrunk on her. You took away her name.

BRAD: What are you talking?

TOMMY: Her name's Sheila. Sheila.

(They turn and see ANDY, by the grave, holding a flower.)

ANDY: Ambulance came and took him. But no surgery needed. They rushed him in. But wheeled him out slow. Shane was gone. Doctor said he lost a lot of blood. But was puzzled. He's pulled worse ones out he said, if they'll just fight. But this guy, he wouldn't. There was no fight in him at all. No fight at all.

I heard that in Beirut some walls are so filled with bullet holes you can just shove your hand through solid brick, it just crumbles into powder. They asked the gunners why they keep shooting even though the enemy's gone. Why they keep killing their own. Why not, they said, we still have plenty of bullets.

Never did suss Shane budding with me. To me he was pure rats on the spine. But it was worth knowing him. Learning the Real. Maybe he was right, me never playing the bad guy. But I get to try. My agent phoned this A.M. I scored the part. Bang bang.

(He puts the flower on the grave. The end.)

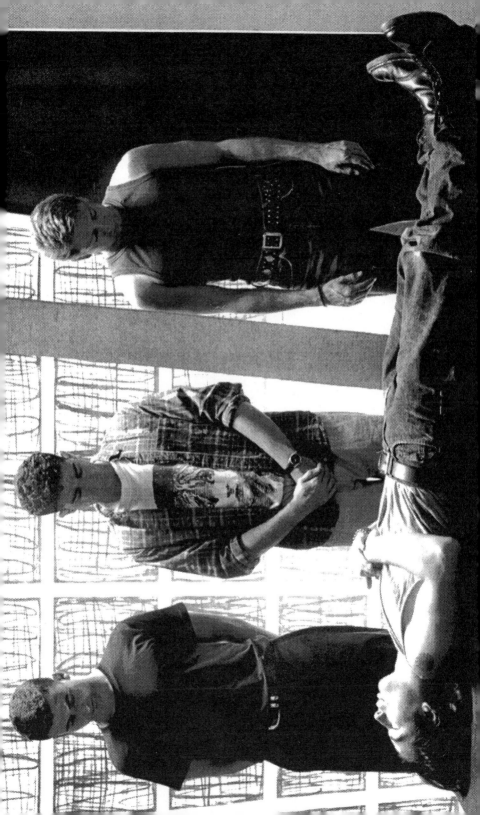

Lying down: Shane (Jacques Lalonde); standing, left to right: Tommy (Marcus Youssef); Andy (Camyar Chai); Brad (Brock Johnson)
Photo by David Cooper